"Kris is a mother to many as she leads a team of hundreds of thousands, but most importantly she's my mom! She leads with integrity and is an expert at vision casting. It's her personal story that led her to build one of the record breaking companies in the Network Marketing profession. I highly recommend this book of you want to be inspired and see what's possible for you."

Sarah Robbins, Author of *Rock Your Network Marketing Business*, Trainer and Top Leader in the Network Marketing

"Kris Fairless I would describe in two words: ALL HEART.

What Kris has written about is not just the power for high achievement in the Direct Sales profession, but for massive success in life powered by the heart. Her story and teaching is a MUST READ for anyone who wants to succeed in a home based business. It will transform your business and life as it already has touched countless numbers of people who have heard her story."

Dr. Doug Firebaugh, Author in the arena of success and leadership, and radio talk show host

D0291749

Assemble Your Team Now!

My personal story of how I assembled one of the top Network Marketing teams built on faith and fearlessness.

by Kris Fairless

Dedication

To my husband, Mark Fairless, thank you for being by my side and supporting me during the good times and the tough times when we were the pioneers leading the multitudes in the trenches and paving the way for those to follow us. You are simply amazing!

Thanks to my daughter, Sarah, as you were the first to say "Yes!" and were by my side during some really hilarious times in the beginning as we literally had to figure out this business by ourselves! I am so incredibly proud of you and how you have grown to be the incredible leader in our company and in our profession.

Thanks to my daughters, Katie and Emily, as you believed in me and always supported my dreams. I am so proud of you both and the entrepreneurial spirit that you both possess.

A very special thanks to my team. I simply could not have achieved what I have done without YOU! It's with love and deep appreciation knowing that you are my biggest supporters and I am yours!

Acknowledgements

I owe much love and thanks to these dear friends who have urged me to get this book out and to be that light and encouragement that someone may need today. I call these friends my "Prayer Generals" because they have been in the trenches of prayer with me praying for our business, our partners and those who would yet join us. Each one of you are incredible and have a huge destiny upon your lives. Thank you to Lisa, Denise, Rachel, Sandra, Jodi and Birgit.

And last, a special thanks to the Founders of our company. You have changed my life and my family's life in a profound way. Today because of you, I get to live out my dream to be the generous giver that I had always imagined. So many are grateful because you are changing lives in ways that prior to this business, I'm sure that you could have only imagined. I have and will always have deep love and respect for you. You are world changers! Thank you!

Table of Contents

Introduction

Assemble Your Team Now
Building Your Network Marketing Team

My goal in writing this book and sharing my strategies with you is based on my desire to coach people to live the life of their dreams and to help them live their lives fearlessly. I know firsthand, since building my own successful direct sales business, the things that this business can provide to those who are willing to launch and diligently work their business. I've watched countless people build successful businesses of their own, and they share specific key traits. I believe that with the right mindset and coaching, you, too, can build a successful business beyond your wildest imagination if you are willing to dream big.

Direct sales companies may not tell you this, but I will: anyone can teach you a system, but what you need to be wildly successful is the right mindset and the unshakable belief that you and your business are worth building. You must believe that your business is worth the cost of your time and the training that it takes to learn your craft. You must also believe that you are worth investing in!

In the building process, you will change many lives as you change your own. Your company should have systems in place to teach you everything you need to know about how to navigate and build your business. I, on the other hand, am here to share with you the things that are essential to becoming wildly successful. Anyone can teach you a system, but I am here to teach you HOW to have the right mindset and HOW to truly believe in yourself, so you CAN accomplish great things. I am living proof that if you engage in the right activity daily, coupled with a lot of perseverance, you absolutely CAN build an incredible business.

My Story

When I was younger and raising our family, I had been looking for a way to provide extra income to our household without doing the typical 9-5. My husband, Mark, and I had three beautiful daughters and my goal was to be the primary caregiver for them.

In today's economy, for many people that's simply not an option. I knew I wanted to be my own boss and create my own schedule so that I could raise my kids on my terms, but the vehicle in which to achieve that goal was elusive to me. I always had an entrepreneurial mind and at one point, my husband and I had even looked at purchasing a franchise that we could work together because my husband didn't love his job as a medical administrator, though it was a means of paying our bills.

Both of us were looking for something that offered flexibility in our day to enjoy our family. We wanted to have the ability and financial means to travel and to live life our way. I had heard of direct sales and network marketing, but, to tell you the truth, I wasn't so sure that was the vehicle I was looking for.

Like a lot of people, I was hesitant to consider a network marketing business to be a legitimate way of providing any substantial income. I had never taken the time to give due diligence to researching the business model until 2005. A friend of mine, Trisha, joined a direct sales business, and in just two and a half short years, she was making $30,000 a month! Can I just say that kind of money caught my attention? Around that same time one of my best friends, Denise, whom I respected, invited me to a meeting where the business Trisha joined was being presented. I must admit I went out of curiosity, because Trisha had formerly held a similar position to mine in a department store as a freelance artist in the world of skincare. Going from $25 an hour to $30,000 monthly, stimulated my curiosity!

As we sat at the table waiting for our guest speaker to arrive, I began to people watch. I have to admit that I was a bit surprised at the caliber of people in attendance. They were far different from my idea of the kind of people who might engage in this business. When Trisha, my former friend and colleague from the world of skincare walked in, I gasped. Quite frankly, I was surprised. I remembered my friend as someone very simple and down to earth, but when I saw her walk in the room that evening I was amazed. There she was, walking towards me, completely transformed by this amazing confidence. In my nervousness as she approached, I couldn't believe what I said to her. "Hi, Trisha. Do you really make $30,000 a month?" After her hello back to me she answered, "Yes, I do."

That was the answer I had been looking for. Here it was in front of me, my vehicle for change. I knew at that moment that the direct sales/ network marketing business channel was the vehicle in which I could be the boss of my schedule and time, plus, create a meaningful income on my terms. If my friend Trisha could do it, so could I!

That evening I joined my friend, Denise, my friend Trisha and countless others in my first direct sales company. Finally, I had a vehicle that would allow me to live life on my terms with no regrets.

The first thing I did when I joined the company was study the business model. For those of you reading this book, if you have not yet done that, I recommend it if you are looking to understand the gift of this business that is in your hands. Instantly, I knew this business model was smart. The model cut out the middleman, who is normally the retailer, and it allowed me to earn the profits for talking about the products directly to the consumer. I loved it! How easy is that? When we love something, it's easy to talk about it!

This type of model saves the company money by allowing consultants to do the advertising for them instead of them hiring pricey ad agencies that create the ads and marketing. In my study of the business, I was impressed that it is one of the most credible business models on the planet. Some of the top financial advisors, economists, authors, and business people in the world endorse network marketing as not only a legitimate business, but also the growing business model of the 21st century. Brilliant business minds such as Warren Buffet, Sir Richard Branson, and

Robert Kiyosaki, to name a few, endorse this business model as a viable profession.

I'm proud to say that I didn't overthink it and I was sold! The only unfortunate part of this story starts with the products that I was sharing at the time when I joined my first direct sales company. Even though others loved them, the products didn't help my skin as I had hoped.

I had something called melasma, which is sun and hormone induced blotchiness on my face. Some women call it pregnancy mask, but the problem was, I wasn't pregnant! The products simply didn't work for me. Although I had a strong conviction in the business model, if you can't believe what you are sharing is beneficial to yourself and others, then you will never grow a successful business. You must believe! I quickly gave that business up, but I never gave up on finding the right company that I could believe in.

In that same year, I started working for a company in the retail setting that had products that actually changed my problematic skin. They were so different from anything else I had ever tried. This line of products contained some over-the-counter medicines and effective cosmetic ingredients that treated various skin care concerns, from sun-damaged skin, to acne, sensitive skin, and aging.

In fact, to tell you the truth, my skin fit into all those categories at one time or another. I was so relieved to unmask from all the heavy layers of foundation that I had been wearing, and for the first time in my life I started receiving compliments on my skin. I was sold on the products and I loved them. I happily worked for this company for two years, not only loving the products, but also loving my job helping people get real results for their skin.

One day, in the spring of 2007, I got a call that I'll never forget. That call forever changed my life. I was standing behind the glass counter in a prestige retail store, when my account executive called me on the phone. She was very direct that day and immediately told me the bad news that I was going to lose my job. Many of you might be able to relate to that kind of messaging, as it was the down turn of the economy in the US in 2007. The company, whose products I was obsessed about, was leaving retail. I was panicked! But I wasn't panicked about losing my income; I couldn't imagine what I'd do if I lost my products. At the time, I was working for about six other skincare companies, so I had lots of products to choose from. However, I couldn't afford to lose the products that did so much for me personally.

Interestingly enough, at that time, I had been praying for a way to make extra income. I wanted to help people in need, but on a greater scale than we had been and I didn't want to be denied in my giving. I always felt that we were called to be generous. After all, what is life all about if we don't help people? Besides having an entrepreneurial spirit, I love giving and personally, I don't want to restrict my generosity because of a balance of my checkbook. There are so many needs in the world, and I have always had a longing and desire to be generous. I didn't want to be

denied in my giving, so I started praying a Scripture
daily that says, "God who supplies seed to the sower
and bread for food will also increase and supply your
store of seed, and will enlarge your harvest of
righteousness. You will be enriched in every way, so
that you can be generous on every occasion and
through us your generosity will result in thanksgiving
to God." (2 Corinthians 9:10-11 NIV)

I knew through my years of serving God and
studying His Word, that God's Word, as we speak it
out loud, does not return to us empty, but it will
accomplish what he desires for the purpose in which
he sends it. (Isaiah 55:11 NIV)

The day my account executive called and told me
the company I loved was taking a leap into the direct
sales industry, I knew immediately that this news was
an answer to my prayer. Remember, I had already
learned that this was a brilliant business model from
my former time in my previous direct sales company.
Within that split second of hearing the news, I had an
inner knowing that I was going to be a multi-
millionaire. I was acutely aware that I was
experiencing the plan that I knew God had for my life
and for the lives of those whom I would yet
encounter.

The first person I called that day was my daughter,
Sarah Robbins. Sarah was a 25-year-old kindergarten
teacher at the time, and like me, she also free-lanced
for skincare companies on the weekends to earn
supplemental income. My call to her sounded like this,
"Sarah, we're going to become millionaires!" I

remember a brief silence on the line before I rushed ahead to tell her that the company with the products that we loved was going to be huge success in this new channel of distribution, and we had the opportunity to be the first distributors. That's how sure I was of the products, the brand and the company. Initially, I told my daughter that we couldn't tell anyone about our new business venture. When we joined the company, it was so new (pre-launch phase) that there wasn't a compensation plan in place yet. My thinking was, if you can't get paid for assembling a team (at the time we could only get paid on the products we sold personally), then why assemble a team? I reasoned that we wouldn't even have the ability to tell people how they could make money, so I told Sarah we could only sell the products ourselves until a compensation plan launched before we could begin assembling a team.

Well, within just three days of that initial call with my daughter, I went to a local church service with a few friends in Ann Arbor, Michigan. There was a special guest speaker that afternoon I wanted to hear, but before he spoke the pastor of the church gave a brief message. Her message was on King David in the Old Testament. King David, before becoming King of Israel, was a humble shepherd boy with no skills in running a nation; but because of his deep love and devotion to God and to doing the right thing, David was divinely appointed as King of Israel. He is described in the Scriptures as "a man after God's own heart." (1 Samuel 13:22-NIV)

Although David was not perfect, he had an amazing faith in God and desired to see God glorified above all else. David was being thrust into his destiny, not by chance, but by God's choice. What I love about this story is it shows that God uses ordinary people who are wholeheartedly obedient and faithful, even in the small things, to carry out His plan and serve others.

As the pastor was sharing the message, she was moving along the front row of the church when she stopped in front of me, pointed her finger at me and said, "There is a destiny that is coming, and this destiny is not singular, but it's corporate. Don't worry how you are going to walk into your destiny because God will align you with those you are to walk into this with." Immediately, chills started covering me, as I knew I had received a word from God. I pulled pen and paper from my purse to write the word down.

We can all share our products, and make sales commission from the products that we are sharing, and that is singular. But to make the bigger money that I wanted for the plans I knew God had for me to accomplish, to help the less fortunate and those in need on this earth, I knew that I had to share this amazing business opportunity with others. As I wrote the pastor's words down, I immediately heard an audible voice. The voice was very loud, authoritative, and commanding. I heard, "Assemble your team," and then in a loud shout, the word "NOW!" It sounded like a male voice, but there were no males sitting around me that afternoon, only women. As I pivoted in my seat to look around to see who shouted at me, I knew that it was God's voice that I heard that day.

My friend Donna, who was sitting next to me, asked me what was wrong, as she saw me pivot in my seat. How could I explain that I had heard God's voice? Without much elaboration as the service continued on, I told her that I heard God speak to me. That was on a Friday, so on Monday, I called the company to ask how I could assemble a team just as the voice instructed me to do.

When I called the company on Monday, it was without any fanfare. The company knew me only as a freelance educator for their company. They had already allowed me to be a part of this new direct sales business the day that I told Sarah. This day that I called them I asked, "How do I assemble a team and how many people do I need to have assembled for you to come out and train us?" There were three people working in the corporate office that day and not many more working for the entire company. They took a few moments to talk to one another and came back on the line to tell me that if I could get 30 people together in a room within a month, they would come out to train us.

The next thing that came out of my mouth actually frightened me, because I said that I would have 100 people gathered together in just a week. I remember the person on the other end of the line saying, "How do you know 100 people?" The answer came so swiftly out of my mouth and without much thought; that I knew it was another affirming word from God passing through my lips. It was a foretelling of what was to come. I told the person that they didn't know my friends and that if I loved something, I would tell my friends and they would tell theirs. True to that word that day, and much to the shock of those on the line, on day seven, with the help of my daughter Sarah and a few close friends, we had 100 people assembled! When the corporate team came out to train us one month after my conversation with them, we had 265 people in attendance at that very first meeting in Michigan and 300 people that had already signed on as consultants.

Initially, I called my best friends and family as I felt this business was too good not to invite those closest to me. I knew this was the business I had always been looking for, and I didn't want anyone that I personally knew to be left behind. I first called my niece, Lisa Smith, a homeschool mom who was also looking for a way to supplement her income.

I then called one of my best friends, Denise Thompson, who had introduced me to the previous direct sales company, which ultimately led me to study this type of business model.

There we were, my initial team of five friends and myself. We started growing a business, which ultimately became a team of a few thousand people before our company ever officially launched.

Who will you offer your business to? You have an incredible gift to offer them because your business has the potential to change their lives! I'm so glad that I shared with those that I cared about and that they said yes, and as a result today, hundreds of thousands of lives have been changed!

Chapter One

Assembling Your Dream -- You

Why

Many people today are looking for something *more* in their life. Some clearly know what they want, and others, unfortunately, have lost their hope for something more. Sadly, because of the reality of their circumstances, some have lost their ability to dream. Others are on the hamster wheel of life, going to work, going home, getting up and doing it all over again. Their weekends are filled with obligations that couldn't fit in during the workweek. Could this be you?

I believe we are meant to live our lives to the fullest and to even enjoy them. I don't believe we were designed to just get through a day and end up feeling exhausted. That's why I know many people are looking for what the direct sales model offers: life on their terms! Many people simply haven't yet discovered that this type of business model exists, or the reality that it actually works!

I know, because this was true for me. Direct sales, the way we sell our products without the middleman, and the way in which we get paid, leverages YOUR time. Goodness knows, with a dream as big as mine, I needed that vehicle to earn extra money without an

ᴐme cap on what I could earn *and* to have total
ᴢxibility in my schedule.

I had always been looking for a way to be my own
boss and to create a life around my passion, which
happened to be my family and giving to those in need.
I finally found this business model that allowed me to
do exactly that.

So, what is your dream? What ignites and inspires
your soul? Finding this out is what will fuel you to take
action. If your *why* doesn't move your emotions, you
won't move either to take action. God has a great plan
of blessing for you and he has a definite purpose for
your life. I assure you that he wants to reveal to you
what that plan is. Take the time with no distractions to
clearly think about what you want. What moves your
soul? What drives you with passion? Is it more money
perhaps to spend more time with those you love? Is it
to travel to see and experience the places that you've
only dreamed of? Is it giving back to people who
need a helping hand? Your dream becomes the core of
your *why*. Without a *why* to propel you forward to live
your destiny you will never really feel completely
fulfilled.

Defining your *why* seems so elementary, yet it's so
crucial for your success. Your reason *why* is your
purpose for building your business, and it's what will
keep you moving forward towards your dream and
your destiny. To discover your *why*, ask yourself,
"What is driving me emotionally to develop a
successful business?"

Your *why* allows you to move towards your dream with laser focus. The power of your *why,* or your purpose, is similar to the energy of light focused through a magnifying glass. Diffused light has little use, but when its energy is concentrated—as through a magnifying glass—that same light can set fire to paper. Focus its energy even more, as with a laser beam, and it has the power to cut through steel. Your why must be clear so that you can have laser focus.

So, let me ask you these questions. If time and money weren't a concern, where would you live? What charities and nonprofits would you give your time and money to? How would you spend your days? Would you create a college fund for your children? Would you pay off debt or possibly buy your dream home and fund your retirement?

My *why*, which I had known was my purpose since my teen years, was to be a generous giver without limits. Before I started my business, it was my joy and pleasure to help people in ways that required money. Even though my husband earned a decent living as a CFO of a large cardiology practice before I was able to retire him from this business, we were just making ends meet. There was no money set aside for retirement, because what little we did have set aside was lost with the downfall of our economy. There was no extra money set aside for my three daughters' weddings, or, for that matter -- and more important at the time -- their college. We borrowed money in the form of home equity loans to pay for student loans and to help our kids buy used, but reliable cars to get them back and forth to school. In my heart I had a burning desire to do more than just get by. I saw people with needs greater than mine, and I wanted to help.

My desire to be generous grew more intense about the time when I was working in the world of skincare as an esthetician. One of my coworkers was in a financial struggle because of failing health. I was impressed to give her a check for a certain amount to help relieve some of her financial burden. At that time my husband oversaw our finances, so I asked him if I could write a check in that amount. Mark was very focused on meeting our budget and suggested that we give a lesser amount. My husband was then and is today a generous man, but he believed that we shouldn't live or give beyond our means. I have to tell you that I was very frustrated that day and not at him, but at our own financial situation. For those who know me well, sometimes when I get very angry I'll cry and I did that day, but out to God. You see, I believed with my whole heart that God had given me this mission or destiny to be generous. I made a decision that day that I wouldn't be denied to the thing I believed God was calling me to. I clearly knew at that moment what fueled me, what gave me passion and purpose and that was to help others in need. I made a decision that day that I would not be denied in my giving and not be limited to the balance in my checkbook!

Because of that decision that day, I am one of the top earners in this company. My husband and myself, along with my daughter and her husband, help people in need all over the world, in particular orphans and widows. My new and improved checkbook helps fund many basic needs for living, such as: building water wells; feeding programs in the US and abroad; helping inner city youth here in the US, and the list goes on. Why am I sharing this with you? Because I want you to catch the vision of what can be possible for you!

I always tell people that your direct sales business is NOT your destiny, but the vehicle to help you achieve it! This is why you must clearly know what your passion is, what fuels your soul and this is what leads you to your why, so that you won't be denied to live the life of your dreams. This business is a vehicle for you to live your best life now!

One of my personal dreams, besides helping people in need, was to travel the world. I wanted to see exotic places and not be confined to trips in the US only. As a result of building my business, I have traveled all over the world. Places like Italy, Paris, Bora Bora, Thailand, England, Australia, Mexico, the South of France, and Spain. As I began writing this book, I was overlooking the beautiful ocean on one of the world's most beautiful islands, Bora Bora, thanks to my incredible company and to the people that I lead. Many people have asked me over the years if my efforts were worth investing my time building this business from the ground up and to that I say, YES! Today it's not just in the way we live traveling the world and seeing the most amazing sights, but the ability to impact and change peoples' lives that moves me. It's the way we can now give that impresses me most about this business and makes my soul sing!

I made many exchanges and some sacrifices in building my business, but I knew those sacrifices would not be required forever. I understood it would take laser focus and a three- to five-year plan for success, so I made my five-year plan and focused on making my dreams come true.

I encourage you right now to make a decision, just as I did. Go ahead. Do it right this minute. Write down your *why*, whether you are doing this for the first time or revitalizing your *why*. It sometimes helps to talk about your plans and goals with your business mentor, which can help you map out your path, which can help you gain greater clarity to fulfill your dream.

If you have clearly defined your *why,* I am going to give you a little exercise to help you bring it into even greater clarity.

Get your vision before you. In scripture there is a verse when it comes to talking about writing a vision and it says, "The LORD answered me: Write the vision; make it plain on tablets, so he may run who reads it. (Habakkuk 2:2 ESV). In order for you to unlock your vision, it's important that you find time to get alone to hear the voice of your Heavenly Father as He wants to speak to you. He wants to give you his heart and his vision for your life. Find a place where you can get time alone with Him where you won't be interrupted. It's hard at times, but try to put away all your distractions like your cell phone and anything that connects you to social media pings. Let your family and friends know that you need silence and not to disturb you. Then write down in as much detail as you can to what you feel He is revealing to you. Write it in the present tense, as though it has already taken place. This step gives you the ability to see your path clearly and then you will have the motivation to walk it out.

You can also visually create your goals by writing them down or by creating a vision board. Have a board that depicts all areas of your life. Find pictures and sayings that represent the things that you want to have in your life. Be creative and find pictures that represent the things that you want. Pull together those things that symbolize an experience or feelings that make you feel happy. Use magazine cutouts, photos of yourself at a happy time and place. Use words and messages of inspiration and affirmation. Find things that inspire you.

Years ago, on a vision board that I made and put in my office, I had   pictures of my dream home in Florida. Today, 7 years later, we are building that dream home! You can do this too and it is so powerful! It can be done on paper, a board or on the Internet, whatever suits your preference. Put this board where you can see it daily to remind you of what it is that you are working for. Visualize daily and dream big! This will increase your belief and keep you moving forward!

Chapter Two

Whatever It Takes – WIT Your Decision to be Successful

I believe that you have everything you need to be successful, even if you are a pioneer in your company like I was. Most companies likely have systems and tools in place for you to plug in to learn your business. I can teach anyone a system to follow, but what I can't give you is the belief to be successful. I hopefully can inspire you to believe in yourself, but that belief comes from deep within you. I truly believe that each one of us has been destined for greatness. It's in your DNA. You were created with a specific purpose upon this earth that only you can fulfill.

Sadly, many individuals never live the lives they were meant to live or accomplish their purpose on this earth, because of fear. Fear is a hindering force, but can be reckoned with. In the Bible there are 365 verses that commands the reader not to fear. In this business, the number one obstacle is fear. There is the fear of being rejected, and fear of being ridiculed by those in your center of influence who are not yet educated on this business model. Then there is the fear of failure, fear of saying the wrong thing, and the fear of approaching people. You can see the list goes on. I personally think what others may think of you is none of your business when you have a destiny to attain.

I was once told that fear is "False Evidence Appearing Real." You are wired to live a life of faith and not fear! The only way to land yourself in the center of your dream is to push past that fear. Have you ever heard the saying, *do the one thing you are afraid of*? Well, I challenge you today to face that one thing. Just do it. The timing will never be perfect, and it is true that not everyone will see what you see. Who cares? Just decide today to live your best life now. You are the one in control. You are the only one who can make change happen. Your faith in what you believe has the power to deactivate the fear if what you believe to be true about your destiny is bigger. There is a scripture that says, "Faith comes by hearing the word of God". (Romans 10:17 KJV)

If you need faith or even more faith about your personal walk into your destiny, then read the Bible, which is the Word of God, where He can speak to you personally and give you what you need to establish truth in your life. Find out who you are in Him and what He has created you to be. Your faith changes things. It gives you the ability to walk out the plan that God has for your life!

When I started my business, I didn't even know how I would get paid. There was no commission plan in place. There were no websites, no marketing materials, and no training. Initially, I didn't even have a mentor to show me the way. Honestly that required great faith! The thing that I did have was great belief --

belief in the brand of products that my company sold, the integrity of our founders, and a huge belief in the direct sales/network marketing industry as a way of building my financial future for myself and my family, and as a vehicle to be able to give charitably to the causes most meaningful to my husband and me.

In the beginning of our company, I made a decision to do whatever it would take to be successful. I call this WIT - Whatever It Takes. Early on, I told my daughter, Sarah, that no matter what we would have to do, we had to make a non-negotiable decision to be successful and to see this thing through. Because the company had not yet launched a compensation plan, I was secretly hoping our company would not roll out as a party plan. I didn't want to leave my home to do parties. However, I was prepared to succeed, even if they had rolled out a party plan. If I had to jump over ten hoops and run through ten barrels, I made a decision that I would do whatever it took and I meant it!

I am not saying it was easy. Being a pioneer in this company without a roadmap was challenging, but because of my decision to do WIT, I was able to weather the storms of a startup company and today live the life that I had only imagined when I first started.

My decision to do whatever it takes (WIT) was far and above the most profound thing I did when launching my business. Quitting or failure was simply not an option! This should be your plan, too, if you are truly looking to change your finances and your life. I have a feeling that if you're still reading this book, this is your goal too.

Chapter Three

Decision vs. Hope

A decision is something concrete. It is not a thought, a wish, or a hope. Often I hear new people come into this business saying they are "hoping" they will succeed. In that case, I tell them that they'll always be hoping. To succeed you must make a decision to do so. With not even knowing how I'd get paid, I made a decision and drew a mental line in the sand to do whatever it would take to learn and succeed in this business. You, too, must make that decision from the very beginning, and that is why having a strong *w hy* in regard to knowing what you want from this business is so important.

There is a learning curve in this business that will take time to master, however, your decision to go the distance is the most powerful gift you can give yourself and your family. This business can change your life and your family's life. You have the ability to compress a 30-40-year career down to 3-5 years. For some it may take longer, but it's the ability to make residual income that speeds up that pace. When I started my business I made a decision to take the five-year path. Because of the time that I took to learn the business model, I didn't overthink the opportunity. I jumped right in and started talking to people to find out what they needed

in their life, and in just five short years into my
business, I had so many more options in my life.
What's equally exciting is that I get to see firsthand the
options that others now have because I said, "yes" to
this business.

I wouldn't quit back then and I won't quit now!
Keep this in your mind that quitting is not an option.
In any decision process, if it's worth having, just know
that you will have challenges and obstacles, and this is
guaranteed. This is called life. I know too many people
who are incredibly talented and have great potential to
do so well in this business but they're not disciplined
about how they spend their time. They have good
intentions but they get easily distracted and off course.
There are a thousand good things that you can give
your time to every single day, but you need to ask
yourself, what are you doing to get closer to your
destiny? You have to stay focused on what's best for
you. If not, you'll get caught up in things that will take
you further away from your destiny. Nothing will be
more sad then getting near to the end of your life and
thinking about all the things you missed seizing that
were right in front of you. Making that decision to go
for your dreams is crucial for your success. Just know
that distractions will come when you're building
something great. Navigating through those distractions
with the right mindset can become your school for
success. You have to stay on course and remain
focused so that you will go to your next level of
promotion because you have a divine assignment
upon your life that only you can carry out.

When you have an assignment on your life to walk out into your destiny, there absolutely will be opposition. The biggest challenge for people in this business is initially getting them past the *no's* that they will encounter. Listen to me... you will get no's and that's a part of this business. Hearing the word NO is actually common in this business. Knowing this upfront can help keep you on course for the long run. If *no* is a part of this business, it's important that you realize the word *no* is not personal rejection. Not everyone will have a need or a desire to do your business, and not everyone will have a need or desire to buy your amazing products-- and that's ok.

I have always told myself from the beginning, and now I tell my team, that you are just a messenger sharing a message of hope and a better life. I liken this process to a waitress pouring coffee. Not all the customers will want the coffee, but she keeps pouring the coffee, unfazed, until the next person says *yes*! Learning to let go of the outcome in the beginning can be a challenge for some, but if you remember that you are simply a messenger sharing a message, and that your job is to help people find out what they want, you'll find those who want your products and will become customers, those who want to be a part of your business, and those who will happily give you referrals.

Today, because I made a decision twelve years ago, I'm free to retire for life if I choose. The residual income this business provides me continues to grow because of the time that I put in upfront, finding people to join me and then teaching them to do the same. My personal goal, however, is to continue to help others achieve their dreams, their goals and to help them walk into their destiny.

Chapter Four

Become a Vision Magnet -- Packaging Your Story

One of the most powerful things you can do in direct sales/network marketing is to become a master storyteller. Learn your story well. Learn about your company, your products, and your personal mission statement. Learn how to package your story. Your company will have outlines on how to share your story. You want to share what your current situation is, what you want to accomplish, and why you've joined. You'll also want to share what your business has done for you.

This is not meant as an opportunity to tell all. You'll want to inform the person you're speaking with about what you are doing and why you are doing it. Let them see how excited you are about what you have already accomplished, and all the things you hope to accomplish. You want this conversation to be short and concise and, above all else, powerful. I call this your Super Bowl commercial. These commercials are short, but powerful. To produce and air the 60-second commercials for Super Bowl Sunday costs companies millions of dollars.

Our society is so inundated with messaging that our attention span is shorter than it has ever been. Let's face it and be real with ourselves; sometimes when we have conversations with people we find them unfocused. They appear to be multitasking in their minds as we speak with them. Is this not true? That's why our message must be short and captivating. With each person you speak to, you have only so much time to capture their attention and engage them.

You also want to be well practiced, so finding someone to practice your story with is valuable. During any chance meeting, you must have your well-practiced story ready so that it will flow freely. There is nothing worse than being stumped about what to say when faced with the unexpected encounter. Practice does make perfect, and at least, it makes you feel more at ease.

I have a personal story about being well practiced that is sure to make you laugh! In the beginning, when my company launched, there were no live or recorded company opportunity calls, so I created the first one. I told my story daily to countless people in person, and I sent my recorded version to all who would listen. My story was so well rehearsed that one day, after having a minor surgery where I had been given anesthesia, I awoke still in a haze from the medicine and found myself trying to bring the nurse-anesthetist into my business.

After my husband and I got in the car and the anesthesia clearly had worn off, I asked my husband if I had tried bringing that woman into our company. He confirmed my suspicions, so I asked him how I did. He said I was amazing, and my messaging was spot on, but he was laughing hysterically because he said I had sounded like I was drugged and of course, I was! That's the power of a well-rehearsed story!

There is nothing more uncomfortable for a potential business partner than over-talking about why you've joined your company. I call this "verbally vomiting" on the person you are speaking with. We've all done it at least once, but from here on in, I don't want any of us to do it ever again. It's painful for us *and* the person we are talking to.

Once you package your story, I want you to hold tight before you start sharing it. In every conversation, the key to your success is first finding out the needs of your prospect. Learning more about them, TINY (Their Interest Not Yours) allows you to know where and how they will fit into your business. Everyone will fit into your business in one of three ways: as your customer, as your potential partner, or as a referral source.

Every now and then someone may not choose to participate, and that's OK, too. You want to engage them with questions that provoke them to go into a conversation of their deepest desires. When was the last time someone asked you about your hopes and dreams? I bet not many people have asked that of you lately. People join you in this business when they like and trust you. You are engaging in a conversation that is building trust; because if people don't trust you, they won't open up to you and so freely share. If you don't know someone intimately, some great questions to ask are, "What do you do"? "What is the best thing about what you do?" "What is the thing you like least?" If you could change one thing about your life, what would your life look like?" "If time and money were of no concern, how would you live your life?" "What do you like to do for fun?"

Once you have accomplished and mastered asking the right questions, you must learn to be quiet and become a great listener. Listening is a key skill that you must perfect to become successful. I know when people in our business will fail, and that's when they can't stop talking. It's a blessing and a curse. Some of the best networkers can talk brilliantly, but they will never build a thriving business if they don't learn to make the conversation about their prospect, and then be quiet and listen intently. You will fail when you make the story all about you and your company without knowing what your prospect needs or wants. Like the game of tennis, there must be that volley back and forth.

Master your story so well that people can relate and then picture themselves traveling a similar journey, based on their need and desires. Remember this: You are a talent scout simply looking for the right new people to join you. Keep their needs in the forefront of your mind.

Remember this acronym that I learned from my friend Doug, many years ago. TINY: Their Interests Not Yours, and you will assemble your own team faster than most.

Chapter Five

Leading People to Their Dreams

Knowing what you want and what you are dreaming for is crucial. We talked about how essential your *why* is in propelling you forward and helping you stay the course. Prospects, those you will be introducing your business to, also have a reason as to why they would consider joining you. Understanding your prospect's *why* is as crucial for their success as it is for your success.

It is said that your *why* should make you cry. My *why* has always been to help people in need and not to be limited to the balance of a checkbook if I saw a need. My *why* was strong, as I would not be denied the call that I believed God put on my life to help others.

When talking with someone, ask yourself, *what is it that this person wants? Do I know clearly what it is?* Finding out takes a lot of detective work and, as I said before, the ability to ask the right questions and listen. Financial freedom and time freedom are not free; there is a cost for both. You must focus and determine if the individual you are talking with has a *why* that is compelling enough to move them forward to join you. Initially, it may not be easy for them to see how your

business can benefit them, but it's so worth it when
they see, and ultimately help them to achieve their
dream.

Your goal is to take your prospects to that place in
their minds where they have been longing and
dreaming to go. Everyone clearly has his or her own
reason for joining you. Perhaps they want more time
freedom to travel, and perhaps your company offers
incentive trips. As long as you paint a picture that
allows your prospects to see themselves on that
incentive trip, it doesn't matter if you have been on
one of the trips yourself or you are presently working
towards winning a trip. It is only possible to speak to
an individual's need or dream if you have discovered
what that need or dream is – and that discovery is the
key in obtaining new partners.

Knowing your *why* and your prospects' *why* in this
business is crucial for your success and theirs. This
business allows you to be entrepreneurial, which is
great on so many levels, because it allows you to
determine how you choose to live your life. However,
many people do not have the staying power to keep
them moving forward daily. My opinion as to why is
because there is not a need great enough in their life
to keep them moving forward.

One of my suggestions for my new partners is to
have them create a goal or vision board of the things
they want to accomplish. I tell them to prominently
display it as a reminder of the things they are working
for. Ask yourself what can be laid aside to open up
your time and resources so you can build something

new. You can accomplish your dreams -- I am here to attest to that. Go for it! You can do anything that you set your mind to if you make a decision to do it.

Chapter Six

Assembling Your Team: It's Not About You - It's About Them

If you are looking to build long-term residual income that can financially set you free, you need to assemble your team. Assembling a team of people creates leverage of your time. When it's just you working your business and selling your products, you are limited by the number of hours in a day. You are a one-man show and it's all about what you do. But when you assemble a team of individuals who want something more in their own lives, true financial freedom possibilities increase exponentially.

When you work alone, you are creating linear income, and that simply means the day you stop working is the day you stop getting paid. In our industry, we get paid residual income, which means we get paid over and over again because we once worked on making the right connections with people who joined us in business.

This creates an army of customer consumers who continue to buy their own products and share them with others long after you introduce it to them. Very much like a recording artist, royalties keep coming in long after the music was first played. I don't know about you, but I know I could only share and sell so many products in one day, but leveraging the time and talents of others who have come alongside me is smart and fun, too. Assembling your team is accomplished by inviting people to join you who are hungry for change and open to possibilities.

There are many people today who may love their professions, but their income -- after taxes and cost of living expenses -- is simply not big enough to sustain them and their families. Some people, if they had a choice, would like to slow down the hamster wheel of life. You know what I mean. Going to work and doing the 9-5 and doing it all over again, day after day. People like you and me are looking for quality of life. After all, we all have only one life to live, and our goal is to make people aware that they do have choices in the way they live.

I have always said that when building your business you initially want to find and bring on your power partner. What does that power partner look like? It can be anyone, and that is why I tell people daily not to prejudge the ones that you will ask to join you. However, with that being said, you are looking for self-motivated individuals, people who have a work ethic and a *why*. These are the ones who are hungry for change and open to possibilities.

You will know who your power partner is. They show up with a twinkle in their eye like my partner, Laurie and her husband, Gary, who I met on a balcony in Italy. I asked Laurie about herself and what she did. As all good games of verbal volleyball go, she asked me what I did, and when she heard that our business had not yet come to Canada, she asked me for the opportunity to join us in business. How did I know she would be my power partner? From day one, Laurie showed up. She was coachable and had a strong work ethic. She never questioned what I asked her to do, but just did it and built an amazing business in Canada.

My daughter Sarah is another one of my power partners, who was an elementary school teacher when she joined me. It was the downturn of the economy in 2007 and Sarah was concerned that she would lose her job due to the turning economy. Her *why* was big, but her work ethic and vision was even bigger. Today she is one of our company's top earners and leaders.

Your ultimate goal, after bringing on your first power partner, is to replicate that process all over again. As I said moments ago, when you assemble a team, you leverage your time and efforts. The key to a successful business is leveraging your time, and in our channel of distribution, you are looking for as many people as possible to accomplish your goal.

The goal for you is to find people who love the idea of living their life on their time and terms. It's also finding individuals who love your products and want to share them. Your partners will have the ability to be their own best customer, and share their results with others. In turn they will sell and service a reasonable number of customers, and then assemble new partners themselves, who will learn to do the same. This is what creates the passive residual income that you continue to get paid on after the initial work is done. Success is building *a network,* or an army of people who are all representing the same products or service, and sharing that success with others.

You need to know this fundamental principle when assembling your team. Your business is about taking people to a place they've been longing and dreaming to go. Building a team is not about you at all. You probably have heard the quote by one of my favorite inspirational authors and speakers, Zig Ziglar, "You can have everything in life you want if you will just help enough other people get what they want."

I found this out for myself two years after I started my business. I had a new friend and business partner in my company, and he had asked me to speak with some of his personal friends at a meeting in Orlando. The meeting was not only to share our business, but for me to share my personal story on how I became a part of this company through a simple prayer and desire to be able to give generously.

I was eager to go to Florida for the meeting, but before leaving, an excited friend called and told me about a post she saw on Facebook. The post said that I was going to share a word about God's principles in the marketplace at a local church in Orlando. I was truly surprised, because I never had intended that to be my message. I wondered what happened to the plan to deliver a message about our business in the marketplace? The thought of the surprise topic was interesting, but I must admit, at that time it was a bit frightening, as well.

I initially had to laugh because I thought that I was possibly the most unqualified person for the topic of speaking about God in business. I came to feel that the Lord was showing me that I was the perfect candidate. I believe God is always looking for ordinary people who are willing to be obedient and have a willing heart to serve Him. After all, if we are believers in Him, are we not to share our faith everywhere we go, even into the marketplace?

I arrived in Florida on a Friday night and the church had about 75 people in attendance. Many were people from my own company. The friend who invited me to speak had assembled a small group of musicians to play some worship music before the meeting ever started. As the music started, one of the musicians called my husband and me out of the audience. He was a drummer who was also a prophetic pastor. He said to us, "Will the couple up front please come forward?" I had shifted around to see if there was another couple sitting up front, but when my husband Mark stepped out, I knew he was talking to us. The pastor said, "I don't know you, but the Lord says that you have a huge marketplace ministry on your lives. You will be taking people to a place that they've been longing and dreaming to go, and when you do this there will be great prosperity, but I'm not talking about just financial prosperity. I am talking about a prospering of their souls and of their dreams. When this occurs, the Lord will literally change their DNA and then their dreams will be fulfilled -- and then the financial prosperity will come. To whom much is given, much is required."

That is our business model in a nutshell. It's taking people to a place that they've been dreaming to go. It's not about us. When we take people to a place of their dreams, then ours will be fulfilled as a result!

So, how do you assemble your team? It's rather simple. I would recommend first pulling out your list of names from your phone, Facebook, and anywhere else you might keep your contacts. If you have a hard time recalling all your contacts, I recommend using a memory jogger. Now if your company doesn't have one, then get your hands on an old-fashioned phone book or find Yellow Pages online. Think of not just the obvious connections, like family and friends, but go deeper.

Who are the people you do business with? This is an often-overlooked list, but an important one, as small business owners are usually looking for extra streams of income. Think of all the places that you frequently spend your money at, such as your hairdresser, your accountant, your dentist, your doctor, your banker, your trainer, and the cashier at your favorite store. You see where I am going.

Next, think about current and former neighbors. Think about the people you went to school with, even all the way back to elementary school.

Think about all the clubs and organizations you currently belong to, or formerly belonged to, and write

them all down. Your goal is to create the biggest list
that you possibly can.

Chapter Seven

Consistency is Key -- Your Daily Activity

Working this business day in and day out like it is a job and not a hobby; will put you on the right path. Now, this is not to say that you can't work your business part-time, as many of you do, and that's great because you can. But did you know that even the top earners in the industry who work the business part-time do it with intention and laser focus? You must have a very specific plan in place! If you don't have a plan, and if you don't work your plan, your dreams will never be fully realized. It's that simple.

A lot of people will fail in this business because they don't have a plan in place. A good way to start your plan is to determine your daily hours of operation. It's so easy to cave into what is comfortable and easy, and let another day pass without tackling that phone call or reaching out to the one who has the potential to change your life and theirs. So, if you haven't already done so, pull out your calendar or click on your digital calendar and take a good look at it. Decide how much time you will devote to your business and how you will spend that time within your business. How many days a week will you work your business, and how many people will you talk with daily? Consistent, daily activity is what matters most.

Talking to people and sharing your story is the activity that will lead you to success. Do you know right now, at this very moment, someone is praying for exactly what you have to offer? If fear and feeling uncomfortable keep you from reaching out, that person will never experience your products or your business. I feel that when we don't share our business we are being selfish. If we joined our company believing in our products and our potential to grow a business, why wouldn't we want to share it? We are simply messengers sharing a message.

When you start working your plan, you are in the process of talking with people about your products and what your business has to offer. If they have no desire for either, you simply ask for referrals. You have an amazing message. You have a gift of hope to offer, the potential for not only financial freedom but also the ability to own your time.

Start today. Identify and write down your priorities. If you don't, it will be easy to fall into old patterns and allow the things that can become time-suckers to take the place of your working hours. Look at your schedule and honestly ask yourself when you can work in your business.

Highlight your working hours and stick to them. Then take massive action tackling your goals and talking to people. Your primary focus should be prospecting (finding people to talk to) and telling your story.

Part of talking to people begins with using your contact list. This list is the heartbeat of your business. It is like gold. I encourage you to keep one list of all the people you have contacted about your business and continue to add to it. This way you can also go back and reference your conversations.

Your goal is to create the biggest list that you possibly can. People will always fall into one of three categories: your customer, your partner, or a source for referrals. Every now and then, people choose not to participate in any way, and that's ok, too. Sometimes they are just watching you and waiting to see your success.

The goal in creating that contact list is not to prejudge whether someone will join you or if they will buy your products. My daughter Sarah and I can attest to this, as the following story pertains to both of us.

My job as a freelancer led me to meet a really great woman who employed me to demonstrate and sell major skincare lines during special events in department stores. I loved working for her and her company. However, when I made my decision to be amongst the first to get involved with the new startup company I am with now, I broke away from the retail setting.

I made a bad decision, and a really bad mistake, by not sharing my new business with my friend and employer of the free-lance staffing agency I worked for. Stacey owned two successful businesses, and her husband was a successful builder. I essentially made a decision for her by deciding she simply would not need or want what I had, because she was way too busy and, in my opinion, did not need the business financially.

My daughter Sarah also knew Stacey, and made the same decision not to ask her for a similar reason. Have you heard of the chicken list? At the time, Sarah was afraid to ask Stacey if she would like to do the business with us because she perceived that she was too successful to approach.

Fast-forward, Stacey was a friend with a lady named Rose. Rose had been a vice president of a major cosmetic brand, but when the economy was in a downturn, she found and joined our new company... and SHE called Stacey.

Rose invited Stacey to have coffee with her because she was looking for referrals and partners to join her, and she could not wait to tell Stacey about her incredible new business.

After Rose shared her story, Stacey asked, "Well, how about me?" No surprise. If you think someone is sharp, most likely someone else does too. Stacey was sharp. She immediately saw the potential for growth and recognized that the timing was right.

Stacey joined Rose, and in that first year of business she became a top recruiter in our company. I still wish I had asked her to join me, but that incident has become a valuable lesson in my business that I share with my partners -- NEVER, EVER, PREJUDGE ANYONE.

You don't know what someone has need of. I didn't know Stacey well enough to know what she was thinking or desiring. People don't wear a sign that tells you what they want or need. Sometimes you simply will not know what they need unless you share the story with them. Remember, if you think someone is great for your business, so will someone else. Don't over-think who you will invite. Just invite them to hear more and let them decide!

You are sifting people through a funnel, trying to see where they fit in. Keep your funnel full because, even if they don't have need for your business, they can become a customer or be a referral source for you. Never, ever quit sharing. I strongly believe that if you connect with the right person who has a need, you will have a new partner or customer, so keep on sharing!

Make it your daily goal to accomplish at least one thing that will move you closer in the direction of your dream. Sharing your story is key; whether that's through social media, a coffee conversation, or simply picking up the phone. Your destiny awaits you. Seize this moment. Go out and share your story, as this business model is truly a gift.

Know that YOU are amazing, and YOU are worth the time and energy it takes to pursue your dreams! You will also discover how rewarding it is to be catalysts in helping others achieve their dreams. In a matter of time, your dreams really can come true. I've seen it happen in my life and the lives of so many on my team!

Let me be absolutely clear on this whole subject matter. Becoming a master storyteller and sharing your story every single day is the most important key to your success.

Chapter Eight

Making Friends

This business is a business of building relationships. It is all about making friends. It's hard to believe, but I think the art of making friends is a dying one. So many of us have become consumed by our own ambitions and agendas that we seldom even make time to be a friend or have a friend.

I feel that to be successful in this business you must be able to connect with people well. For some of you this comes naturally, and for others this may be difficult. I actually know a top income producer in another company who says that he is such an introvert that he will turn away from you on an airplane and stick his nose in a book. Fortunately for him, though, he can turn his people skills on at his will and does so to build his business.

For me, I love people, and meeting them comes quite easily to me, but for those of you who may be challenged, I am going to give you a lesson on how to make new friends. You might be laughing right now and asking out loud, "Really?" and I say "Yes, really!" Our business, done well, is a business of building relationships. People join you when they know, like, and trust you. Too often, however, we are so excited about the prospect of recruiting, we make it all about us and our products or opportunity. WRONG PLAN! You have heard me say many times, and it bears repeating, TINY: Their Interest Not Yours. Finding out about what your prospect wants and needs is the key to your recruiting success.

There is only one way to get anyone to do anything and that is by helping that person want to do it. The only way I can get you to do anything is by giving you what you want. So why is it, then, so many of us when telling our story, sharing all the great features and benefits, don't see more people join us? You saw it and you joined! Why then don't our friends and family see this great business as an opportunity for themselves? Have you ever considered that maybe you've shared all the great selling features that you were attracted to? Hmm…. You know it's not about you but it's about them! Henry Ford said, "If there is any one secret of success, it lies in the ability to get to the other person's point of view and see things from that person's angle as well as from your own." The way to get people to join you is to be genuinely interested in them. After all, it is all about them!

One of my favorite books that I will reference in this chapter and is a must-read is How to Win Friends and Influence People by Dale Carnegie. Our business is all about personal self-development and developing relationships. Dale Carnegie says that when we attempt to force change onto people, we almost always fail, but if we can take the time to see the problem from the other person's perspective, and then help that same person understand how the improvement will actually benefit them, we have a much better chance of success. We have to engage our prospect and help them acquire an eager want. I call that hungry.

Let's key into some practical techniques of prospecting with your prospect being the focal point, not your business. First, let's connect with the person's name. One of my favorite friends, an expert in our industry for over thirty years, became a mentor to me in the beginning of my business. His name is Doug.

Initially, I had no clue what I was doing, but I had built a large team of personal partners because I already had a lot of the necessary relational skill sets down. My friend Doug did a training for my first batch of new partners, and it was immediately apparent why he was so successful in this profession - his people skills are off the charts! When you are in a room with Doug, he makes you feel as if you are the most important person in that room.

As he was doing that training, he referenced my name several times and he made eye contact directly with his audience and me. He asked others their names, too, and he remembered them. He asked a lot of questions about the individuals he was training. It was from him that I learned the acronym TINY: Their Interest Not Yours. Doug was -- and is -- a master of relationships.

Let's start with what Doug did well. I was impressed by his ability to connect by using our names. People REALLY value you calling them by name. So, if you reconnect with someone you've met before and don't remember his or her name, you're not starting off well. Many politicians are incredible at remembering names... some go as far as to jot people's names down in their phone after they meet them so they have a better chance of recalling that person's name later. Make it a practice to call people by their name. For example, if I'm talking to my friend Emily, I might start the conversation with, "Hey, Emily...how's it going?" instead of, "Hey, how's it going?" So, do your best to remember names...write them down if needed, and then try to call people by their name at least twice the next time you have a conversation with them to make it stick. Remember that a person's name is to that person the sweetest and most important sound in any language.

Another thing that I noted about my friend Doug is his ability to listen. Listening well is a gift that we give someone. Tell me -- when was the last time you felt someone really listened to you? Hopefully, it hasn't been that long, but for many of us those types of conversations are few and far between.

So often we have our own agenda and time is at a premium. In order to accomplish our agenda of sharing about our business, we can barely wait until the person gets through speaking so we can jump in. Does that sound familiar? If you want to be a good conversationalist and have people enjoy being around you, you must be an attentive listener. To be interesting and likeable to someone, you HAVE to be interested in them. Remember, people join you in this business when they like and trust you.

Now here are some practical tips for establishing a friendship. You need to get to know people. How do you do that? Start by asking questions that people will enjoy answering; encourage them to talk about themselves and their accomplishments. I call these ice-breakers. "So, what do you do for a living and do you like what you do? How long have you been there? What's the best part of your job? What do you like least? How many kids do you have? I know raising kids can be expensive. What do you and your family like to do for fun?" Your goal is to listen closely to what they say. Pay attention. Find out in the conversation where your opportunity can fit into their life.

Be a great listener while encouraging others to talk. When I get people on a call with me, I ask them if time or money weren't a concern, how would they like to spend their time. One woman once told me how she loved to travel, but she had no time and very little extra money. Believe me, one of the primary things I focused on when sharing my business was our company's free, all-expense-paid trip! I painted the pictures of Bora Bora, Thailand, Paris, and Italy. What do you think she did at the end of our conversation? She asked me what it took to get started! That is the reason you should encourage people to talk about themselves.

Find out what people are interested in and direct your conversation towards that topic. Now, to some this may sound obvious...but a key aspect to building rapport with people is to find ways to connect with them.

Pay people sincere compliments. This is huge. I am not talking phony compliments, but sincere ones. If you compliment them, it is another way to build rapport and get them to open up about themselves.

When someone talks to you, look at them. This may sound obvious, but if you're more interested in looking at your phone while "talking" to someone, chances are you're not being a good listener. Look people in the eyes and smile. Simply put, actions speak louder than words, and one of the most powerful actions any of us can take is to smile. Yep, simply smile.

Dale Carnegie explains in his book that a smile says, "I like you. You make me happy. I'm glad to see you." I encourage you to do your very best to really smile...and not just make an insincere grin. With this said, even if you don't feel like smiling, you should force yourself to smile. Act as if you are already happy, and that will tend to actually make you happy, or at least happier. In fact, Psychologist William James once said, "Action seems to follow feeling, but really, action and feeling go together... thus the sovereign voluntary path to cheerfulness...is to sit up cheerfully and to act and speak as if cheerfulness was already there..." Another interesting point is how important it is to smile, even when you're talking to people on the phone. It comes through!

Make the other person feel important – and do it sincerely. If you have done all of the above getting to know someone and what their likes and interests are, you are on your way to developing a friendship and, quite possibly, someone to join you on your journey!

Chapter Nine

Assembling Your Words and Conversations

There is power in your words. Whether good or bad, words can set the course for your life. I believe that the life I am living today is a direct result of the things that I have spoken over myself. Like you, I am a work in progress. I am far from perfect, but I am always diligently watching what I speak about myself. I even consider what I am speaking about others. There is a scripture in the Bible found in Proverbs verse 18:21 KJV that states, "The tongue can produce life or death and those who love to talk will reap the consequences." The words that we speak are like seeds that can produce a great and plentiful harvest of good things in our life -- or disaster. For that reason, I am very careful to watch my words.

When I shared my business opportunity with my daughter, Sarah, who was my first business partner, I told her we would become millionaires. There was never any wavering or doubt of what we would accomplish.

At the time, though, I didn't know exactly what that journey would look like. We had no blueprint to follow. There was no roadmap to the 'millionaire mile'.

The amount of time that it would take to build my dream didn't matter to me, because I had only one clear objective, and that was to share a message of hope knowing that God would align me with the right people who had dreams of their own. My goal was to take them on this journey with me and together we would change lives.

So, let's begin to examine what you are saying with your words. Do you believe for good things to happen in your life, but then the opposite comes out of your mouth? Do you want to build a successful business and have the things that you desire, but are you telling people the opposite?

I once had a partner in business who told me that she wanted her business to grow. She then proceeded to tell me all the things she was doing to make it happen. It seemed like she was engaged in the right activity, but when she spoke, her words didn't line up with her desires. She was saying things like, "I have no clue what I am doing wrong. I am doing all the right things, but I never get ahead. I can't get anyone to join my business for the life of me. It's just my small team and me and we're struggling just to get our titles monthly. This is just a struggle for me, and I don't know if it's worth it." And so it was a struggle.

The repeated conversations almost always had a tone of defeat. How did this person see herself? As one who would never get ahead, because this is what her heart told her was true. She was defeated because the overflow of her heart was coming out of her mouth. It was horrible to watch, and seemingly impossible to stop, even though I pointed out what she was saying to be destructive.

There truly is great power in your words. You cannot talk defeat and expect to have victory in your life. There is a Scripture in the Bible (James 3:2-12 NIV) that tells us the tongue is like a bit in a horse's mouth, or a rudder on a ship that steers the vessel. The apostle James also said that the tongue "sets the whole course of one's life on fire." Our words have the ability to bless or curse our lives, and to create life or release death (negative circumstances) into our life. The tongue – our words – has the ability to set the direction of your life. I believe that your life today is a direct result of your words that you have spoken over yourself or those who have spoken over you. You can literally speak blessings over your life or curses that bring destruction.

Today I am blessed because I have spoken blessings over my life and not curses. I have spoken favor and not defeat. My husband and children are blessed because of God's goodness and the words that have been spoken and prayed over them daily. The Bible that I read to encourage and guide my life is like an instruction manual for daily living that says, "I am the head and not the tail. The actual scripture verse says, the Lord will make you the head, not the tail. If you pay attention to the commands of the LORD your God that I give you this day and carefully follow them, you will always be at the top, never at the bottom. (Deuteronomy 28:13 NIV) I also declare (Deuteronomy 28:6 NIV) that I am blessed as I go in and blessed as I go out. My favorite that I declare daily is, "The blessing of the Lord makes one rich, and He adds no sorrow with it". (Proverbs 10:22 NKJV)

If you are telling yourself, "I will never get ahead," watch how you will never get ahead. If you are saying, "I never get good breaks," watch how that statement becomes true. Are you speaking what you desire? My daughter, Sarah Robbins, writes in her book, Rock Your Network Marketing Business, her story about when she was brand new in our business and building her team. She went from saying things like, "I'm young, so nobody will join me," to words of "I am a top earner" and "I have the fastest-growing team in the company." At the beginning of every personal team call, she spoke the words that they had the fastest-growing team in the company, even at the time when it wasn't true, but I saw it happen right before my own eyes. Her words became a fact. Your words will align you with your destiny, so what are you saying about yourself? If you are not where you want to be today, ask yourself *what am I speaking over myself and my life and business? Is it blessings or curses?* Are you speaking good things or bad? It's up to you, but I challenge you to speak boldly over yourself, your family, and your business, and watch how things will come to pass.

I want you to remember this; you were made in the image and likeness of God. If God had the creative power to form the Heavens and the Earth with His words and you are created in His likeness, then you have that same power in your words! It is also written: "I believed; therefore I have spoken." Since we have that same spirit of faith, we also believe and therefore we speak. (2 Corinthians 4:13 NIV)

You see, I deeply believe that we are spirit-beings created in the likeness and image of God, Himself. If we are created in His likeness and image, then we have the same power that resides in us to change our world through our words. Your words create your future, so make a decision today to keep yourself fixed on what God says about you.

I really encourage you to receive what I am saying and to watch what happens when you not only read God's Word, but also speak His Word over your life daily. Let His words sink deep into your heart and mind so they become a reality.

Here are some scripture verses for you to speak over yourself to prosper yourself and your business. A great scripture that affirms what I'm saying is, "You shall decree a thing (or speak a thing) and it shall be established and light shall shine upon your ways". Job 22:28 (WEB)

Jeremiah 29:11-13 (NIV) "For I know the plans I have for you," declares the Lord, "plans to prosper you and not to harm you, plans to give you hope and a future. Then you will call on me and come and pray to me, and I will listen to you. You will seek me and find me when you seek me with all your heart." In order to have a successful business, you must trust in the Lord. I thank the Lord daily for his goodness and faithfulness, because I know His plan is to bless and prosper me.

Proverbs 16:3 (NIV) "Commit to the Lord whatever you do, and he will establish your plans".

Daily I ask the Lord to order my steps, even from the pitfall of possible distractions. I ask that He would align my steps to the people He would have me connect with.

Isaiah 54:2-3 (NIV) "Enlarge the place of your tent, stretch your tent curtains wide, do not hold back; lengthen your cords, strengthen your stakes. For you will spread out to the right and to the left; your descendants will dispossess nations and settle in their desolate cities".

I thank the Lord that my territories would be enlarged. I believe that I have influence and you can have influence in your business, too. Your business is a marketplace ministry to show God's love to others, even as you build it in other nations.

Isaiah 30:21 (ESV) "And your ears shall hear a word behind you, saying, "This is the way, walk in it," when you turn to the right or when you turn to the left". Daily I ask the Lord that I would hear His voice regarding my decisions.

Philippians 4:19 (NIV) "My God will meet all your needs according to the riches of his glory in Christ Jesus".

I thank God that He meets all my needs for the day.

Proverbs 10:22 (NIV) "The blessing of the Lord brings wealth, without painful toil for it".

Proverbs 3:4 NIV "Then you will win favor and a good name in the sight of God and man.

I declare that the blessing of the Lord is upon me and that He causes me to have His favor daily in the sight of God and man.

Here is a sample of what I pray daily over myself and my business that you can use too, to bless your life, your business and your partners.

Father I thank you that your plans are to bless and prosper me today and to give me a hope and a future. I commit my way to you today, Lord. Please order my steps and those of my partners. Father, I pray for my business and my business partners today. Enlarge our territories and cause us to grow even to dispossess nations. Allow me to hear your voice today as you speak to me and tell me the way that I am to go. Thank you, Father, that you meet all my needs according to your riches and glory. Thank you that you give me favor in the sight of God and man and that you, Lord, cause your blessings to overwhelm and overtake me today. Amen

Chapter Ten

Assembling Your Plan:
It's a 3-5-year Plan and it's Not Get Rich Quick

To achieve success you must have a plan. If I told you that this business was one where you would get rich quick, you'd be frightened. I'd be frightened for you if someone told you that. Like any business, it takes sweat equity of your time to build. Traditional business, in many cases, takes about five years just to break even. In our business, you have the potential to create a 30-40-year career in three to five years. You make upfront income by simply sharing and selling your products, but you have the possibility of creating wealth that you've only dreamed of by building a team. So how did I find out that this business model takes 3-5 years to build? It began as a result of my quiet time.

Before I plan each day, I know that according to the instruction book for my life, the Scripture in Psalms 37:23 NSV, says, "The LORD directs the steps of the godly. He delights in every detail of their lives".

I encourage you to spend some quiet time with God to hear what your course needs to be. I personally know that I get strategies for my life and my business when I spend a few minutes of quiet reflection and meditation with the Lord each day before I get busy.

This is the problem for most of us. We are way too busy doing something at every moment in our day. For some of you, this time of meditation is no easy task, with all the commitments you have, including your family. I will tell you, however, that it is worth it to carve out that quiet time to be still and listen.

You've probably already figured it out, but we are not designed to be *doing* all the time. You are a human *being*, and just "being" is something that is all too often neglected in our busy lives. Nelson Mandela once said, "I'm too busy today NOT to spend an hour on my knees." When you are in a state of just *being*, you will often find answers to the problems that have been perplexing you. In the quiet, reflective place, you will receive God-given downloads about what you need to do next. Your strategy and plan will come. You will have moments of clarity and certainty. You will become aligned with who you truly are, and what you truly want, need, and are worthy of. Take time daily to meditate, to be quiet and just listen. God wants to speak to you. Take at least 20 minutes a day just to be quiet with no one else around. Listen and allow yourself to daydream. Allow yourself to relax your body, mind, soul and spirit, and allow yourself to just be. If you've never done that before, I highly recommend that you try it. You'll be surprised at the things you might hear and the thoughts that will freely come to give you direction.

One morning, early on in my business before our company launched, I was about to rush into my morning but knew that I needed first to pray and be quiet to listen for direction. I remember the feeling distinctly of being overwhelmed with all the meetings that I had planned for that day. My simple prayer went something like this, "Dear Father, I'm already tired and I haven't even started my day. I'm feeling a bit overwhelmed with all that I need to do today. Please show me what you would have me do. Thank you."

Within a second of that prayer request, I had a distinct impression that gave me clarity. It was at the beginning of the downfall of our economy and the State of Michigan, where I live, was already being hit hard because most of our commerce is tied to the automotive industry. I was impressed to attend a meeting I had read about in an email sent to me a day earlier from a church that I had never attended.

The email said, "If you know of anyone who needs a job within the State of Michigan, or if you have one to offer, please attend this meeting." I had read the email, but had never given a second thought to going and presenting my business. Frankly, I was too tired trying to figure out how to build my business as a pioneer without a road map. Because the thought came to me so quickly, I acknowledged that I needed to go, but through the course of my day presenting my new business to friends, I forgot about my commitment until 6:00 PM that evening.

I was just pulling up to my driveway to get my mail. When I pulled the mail out of the box, there was a big stack with one letter on top of the pile that stood out. It was from the church that I had committed to attend that night. I knew it was a reminder -- or a sign, if you will -- of my commitment to attend. When I opened the letter I was dumbfounded.

The letter was a thank you. It was a thank you addressed to my husband and me for our recent contribution of $410. 00. Well, I was shocked, as I had never given $410 to that church and, as far as I knew, neither had my husband.

I went in the house and began dinner for our family. When my husband walked in, I told him about the letter we received and asked him if he had given $410.00 to that church. He said, "no", just as I thought he would. My next question was, "Have you recently given any church $410.00?" Once again, his answer was "no."

That was all I needed to hand my husband his dinner and jump in the car and drive off. I drove about 30 minutes to the church, or so I thought. The address took me to the pastor's home. Remember, I had never been to the church before. I went to the door where I saw about 35 people gathered in the living room. I nervously knocked on the door and was led inside by a friendly, smiling person. I sat down in a chair, not knowing a soul there.

The pastor was talking about a destiny that would come to Michigan. Something that people would be talking about that would boost people's income in

Michigan, and people would say when the opportunity came to them, "Why Michigan?"

After the pastor was done speaking, I raised my hand to introduce myself to the strangers in the room. I said something along the lines of, "Hi, I'm Kris Fairless, and God brought me here." I know there were a few laughs, as it was the unexpected thing to say or to hear, but that was the truth. I told my story of how I woke up and prayed and had the immediate thought that I was to attend this meeting. I then mentioned the letter of thanks for the donation of $410.00. I felt led to say to the pastor that I felt they had a need for that $410, and that I would give them a check the next evening.

I also shared my story of how my business came to me and how I heard God's voice say, "Assemble your team now." After the meeting was over, the pastor said, "I will call you in the morning," and she did. Bright and early at 8:00 AM, she called me and told me she wanted to join my team and she wanted me to meet a good friend of hers who was an expert in this industry.

Needless to say, I signed this pastor, named Kim, into my business and she introduced both me and my daughter Sarah to our now friend, Doug Firebaugh, whom I told you about earlier and had become a friend and mentor to us when we had none in our beginning days.

Doug met us at Panera Bread that day in Novi, Michigan. I will never forget what he was wearing, a pair of jeans and a Detroit Tigers baseball cap. We introduced ourselves, and Doug asked me to tell him my story. I explained about our opportunity and the timing to be amongst the first in the business.

I know why I so clearly remember what he was wearing that day, because when I was done telling him our story he sat up very straight and pushed his ball cap to the back of his head and said, "Dear Lord, you have no clue what you have here, because if you did, you wouldn't be sleeping at night."

I did realize what I had and Doug was right... I already was not sleeping. I got the magnitude of the opportunity -- as he said, "Your Company is so rich in culture (meaning the founders had already created another brand with huge recognition and credibility) and it's at the perfect timing (the opportunity to be amongst the first). He said, "Don't overthink this. You go out and tell everyone you know. Work this business for the next 18-24 months, consistently talking to people, and in three to five years you will have the potential to retire for life."

At the time, I was 48 years old and I remember thinking *five years goes in a blink of an eye. I can do anything for five years,* and five years was my benchmark. True to what he told me, I was able to retire my husband 14 years early in just two years time from his company because I had tripled his six-figure income as a CFO. In just three years, my daughter and I became the first seven-figure earners in the company.

So, what is my point in telling you this hard-to-believe, but true, story? We have our plans, but it is so much better to seek wisdom about those plans. That one detour in my day became a divine connection that we were to have in order to ground me in the right mindset. This business has the potential to change your life and to set you financially free, but it doesn't happen overnight, and that is why having minimally a 3-5 year plan is a realistic goal.

Chapter Eleven

Be Fearless- Believe in You

Everything in this business that would help you succeed is wrapped around your belief. To start, you have to believe in our business model, which is direct to consumer marketing. It's so smart cutting out the middleman. You also have to believe in the products that you represent by using them and falling in love with them. There is nothing more powerful than a true testimonial of sharing your own results. Then there is one last thing that you must have belief in, and that's YOU! This is the one area where I find people struggle the most. You have to know beyond a shadow of a doubt that you were destined for greatness before the beginning of time. Knowing your purpose and God's plan for your life has already been written out in advance is the first key to this belief. You have been equipped in advance with everything you need to be successful.

There is great passage in the Bible about a man named Gideon. There was a great distress amongst his people, the Israelites, and they were distressed because of the oppression of their enemy the Midianites. They were so distressed and oppressed that they were hiding in the caves.

Gideon threshed wheat in the winepress, in order to hide it from the Midianites. And the Angel of the Lord appeared to him, and said to him, "The Lord is with you, you mighty man of valor!"

Gideon said to Him, "Oh my lord, if the Lord is with us, why then has all this happened to us? And where are all His miracles which our fathers told us about, saying, 'Did not the Lord bring us up from Egypt?' But now the Lord has forsaken us and delivered us into the hands of the Midianites." Then the Lord turned to him and said, "Go in this might of yours, and you shall save Israel from the hand of the Midianites. Have I not sent you?" So he said to Him, "Oh my Lord, how can I save Israel? Indeed my clan is the weakest in Manasseh, and I am the least in my father's house." And the Lord said to him, "Surely I will be with you, and you shall defeat the Midianites as one man." (Judges 6:11-16 NKJV)

This is a perfect example of how we sometimes see ourselves and yet, how God sees us. Sometimes we see ourselves incapable of launching our dream. Like Gideon, we like to play it safe, not risking stepping out into the unknown. We make excuses as why we aren't able to accomplish our destiny before we ever launch it. Gideon thought that he was too young and his family was too poor. God saw Gideon as competent to do the job. Even though Gideon felt fearful and saw himself as incompetent, God saw him as fearless and bold.

If you believe that you aren't enough or you don't have enough, you will continually be operating in scarcity in every area of your life. Just know that God sees you as He created you. There are no limits and there is no lack. He has a specific purpose and plan in place for you. The Lord sees you fully equipped and ready to do whatever he has called you to do. I urge you to be bold and know that you playing it small doesn't serve you and the world that is waiting for your story. Your life and your very existence is a message to the world. Remember that!

Being fearless is a choice you have to make everyday about your business. It's much easier to make excuses and say your business is not working for you when people aren't joining you. Remember you're more than average. You are a Child of the King. There are building blocks to this business, and you may be in the place of perfecting your craft. Remember, there is no personal rejection when someone tells you no. Timing truly is everything, and over time and in their time, you will grow your team. Resilience and grit is an essential key in assembling your team, but you can do it!

Many of you reading this book may be thinking, well Kris, this all sounds great but it's not easy for me to put myself out there and be vulnerable. Believe me I know. I am no different than you. I have experienced those voices of self-doubt at times, too.

I believe at one time or another, we all have doubted our ability to accomplish something noteworthy.

For instance, in writing this book. I actually wrote this book about five years ago, but I didn't get it out after initially writing it because I questioned who would read it. After all, I have no formal degree in writing. This wasn't even my thought to write a book in the first place to be totally honest. Let me tell you what I mean.

Getting this book out has been a challenge for me. Thoughts of its insignificance plagued me until one night I had fallen asleep and woke up with the television on. At the exact moment I woke, a Pastor named Joel Osteen came on and said, "Some of you are being disobedient to the thing that God has called you to. Your obedience or disobedience will affect future generations." He then told the story about his father who had built Lakewood Church, which is the church Joel now pastors. Back in the day, when his church was established, his dad felt like it was time to build a bigger church. It took several millions of dollars in fundraising efforts to build that church and when he had gathered that specific amount he felt an impression in his heart to give it away to another church. You can imagine that he argued his case on that one, but finally out of obedience he gave the money to that church. When Joel's Father passed away, Joel took Lakewood church over and became the Pastor. The church attendance grew even bigger. It was time to move on and Joel had his sights on the former Compaq arena in Houston Texas, which is a 16,800-seat auditorium. On the day that they were moving into the new arena, Joel spotted a big sign on the road as he was driving there from the church his

Father gave the money to years ago and it said something like, 'Thank you Lakewood Church for our humble beginnings". Joel said that he knew his father's obedience was the result of the new church they were entering into. From humble beginnings to now one of the largest churches in the United States.

After watching that segment at approximately at 1:15 AM, I talked to the Lord. "God, if that is really you speaking to me, please give me a confirmation within 24 hours." I felt relieved, to be honest, to go all day long without having the message confirmed to me. I went to bed and exactly 24 hours later to the exact minute, I woke up once again at the exact time, 1:15 AM. I heard that familiar voice saying, "Some of you are being disobedient to the thing that God has called you to". That was a clear sign that I was to write this book. This book isn't for fame or fortune, but to be a blessing in someone else's life.

Now the story would be great if I told you I completed that book two years ago as instructed, but I kept listening to the lies. I thought this is just my story, who will want to read it? Two years later and a after a good talking to from a dear friend, I realized that my story, even if it's for one person, to step out in faith and accomplish the hard things. Maybe that is simply to strengthen your faith to trust God for bigger things and to believe that if I could do this business with no former experience and become successful, so can you!

You have a destiny on your life. It will require obedience to fulfill it. It will take work and some hustle and in some cases, a lot of hustle. It will take some sacrifices too, to live the life of your dreams. You are meant for greatness. Remember Gideon? When Gideon obeyed God, even against the odds, he ended up in victory!

Be fearless in the pursuit of your dreams. I know that someone is waiting on you to help them change his or her own life, as you change yours! I believe in you. You can do this if you believe that you are who God says you are. You are loved, you are blessed, you are forgiven, and you are whole in every area of your life. Keep your eyes on your dream and never ever give up. God's got a specific purpose in mind just for you.

Life is so rewarding when you have the realization that YOU can be the answer to someone's prayer! Someone is counting on you, so go ahead and "Assemble Your Team Now"! Great things lie ahead for those who do. Your story is waiting to be told!

About the Author

Kris Fairless is passionate about taking people to a place that they have been longing and dreaming to go. Kris shares with her readers' specific strategies to help them assemble and build their own Direct Sales/Network Marketing Team. Kris's story is one of faith and perseverance leading the charge in a company that was so brand new it was still a secret to the nation. Kris was fueled by a desire to be generous to people in dire need around the world and God answered her prayer. Read as she shares with you how she assembled and built a team that now has grown into an icon in the industry creating a seven figure annual income for herself and her husband Mark in 3 years time. Today that income has fueled their passion to be the givers that they always dreamed they would be.

Contact Kris at KrisFairless.com.